CONTENTS

The *virtual organisation*, it has been suggested, is the organisation of tomorrow. The concept embraces a range of flexible working practices facilitated by new communications technologies. Companies will come to see themselves not as fixed structures but as networks of resources to be assembled and disassembled according to need and irrespective of physical location. Although it can be argued that elements of the virtual organisation have existed before in terms of, for example, outsourcing and homeworking, only now is a coherent, more widespread model emerging. This development is based on three fundamental factors:

1 The organisational structures and management concepts of the past are no longer viable in a marketplace of rapid and continuous change.
2 The ability to respond to such change requires a new flexibility which affects our traditional ideas of organisation and management.
3 Technologies which were formerly separate and distinct are now converging to support the flexibility demanded by organisations.

Understanding the Virtual Organisation in a Week aims to introduce managers to the trends leading to the creation of the virtual organisation, as well as to concentrate on the better-known aspects of the concept, such as teleworking, outsourcing and strategic partnerships, which are in use today.

What is the virtual organisation?

We have identified 10 questions to help understand the overall concept of the virtual organisation. Today we shall deal with each of these in turn.

1 How is the virtual organisation defined?
2 How does it apply to organisations today?
3 What will the organisation of tomorrow look like?
4 When will this change take place?
5 Why is it happening?
6 What might slow it down?
7 How will it affect the way I work?
8 What are the benefits?
9 What are the dangers?
10 Why do I need to bother with virtuality?

How is the virtual organisation defined?

Whatever the virtual corporation turns out to be, flexibility will be its defining characteristic.

Society of Management Accountants of Canada

Information will be the core of the virtual corporation.

Davidow and Malone

Virtual organizations ... do not need to have all the people, or sometimes any of the people, in one place in order to deliver their service. The organization exists but you can't see it. It is a network not an office.

Charles Handy

A temporary network of independent companies linked by information technology to share skills, costs and access to one another's markets.

International Business Week

Virtual organizations will be reliant on the medium of cyberspace; will be enabled via new computing and communications developments; [and] will initially only exist across conventional organizational structures.

Christopher Barnatt

As we can see, there is no single definition of the virtual organisation. In this book, however, we shall use it as a term which brings together the various initiatives, such as teleworking, outsourcing and strategic partnerships, which organisations are exploring to make themselves more responsive to changes in today's marketplace. We shall also use the term to indicate a hidden reality behind the scenes, where results are not achieved in traditional ways. It describes the notion that an organisation, team, individual, or even a product or service, is not *physically present*, even if it may *appear* to be so, and is thus, in a sense, both real and not real in the customer's perception.

All writers do at least agree that the concept has a number of key characteristics:

- *It is facilitated by the use of telecommunications technologies.* Computing and telecommunications technologies have converged to allow desktop computer systems to become interconnected for data exchange between individuals who are physically remote from one another. The electronic environment within and across computer and communications systems, and in which information is shared, is known as *cyberspace*, a term coined by the futuristic writer William Gibson in his novel *Neuromancer* (New York: Ace Books, 1984).
- *It harnesses various forms of organisational flexibility*, unconstrained by the traditional barriers of place and time. This process involves practices such as cross-functional teams, outsourcing, and teleworking *within* organisations, and strategic partnerships and temporary alliances *between* organisations.
- *It demands a greater level of trust* because people will be working out of sight of their co-workers and managers for the majority of the time. This impacts on the relationship between employer and employee, and it similarly affects business relationships between one organisation and another.

How does it apply to organisations today?

It can be argued that the virtual organisation, stripped of its technological aspect, has always existed. Good examples here are those small companies that have a unique, clear identity on paper but no premises to match. For example, the owner may work at home, using a spare bedroom as an office, or on a customer's premises, or in a car, touring around to win business. They may employ a secretary who works from home, and they may also subcontract work when necessary. Larger organisations have often employed homeworkers, and are used to employing sales teams who spend most of their time away from the office, on their own and out of sight of their employer. Peripheral activities, such as catering or car-fleet management, have been outsourced for many years, and some companies, such as Nike and Marks & Spencer, have built their success on outsourcing most or all of their manufacturing, concentrating on their core competence of marketing. The number of strategic partnerships is also growing, and even the idea of temporary alliances where companies come together with other organisations for specific projects is not new – take the movie, publishing and fashion industries, for example.

What *is* new, however, is that technology is now allowing such activities both to become easier and to expand. It is now possible for people to share information and to keep in touch quickly and conveniently. Barriers of distance and time, which in the past have created unacceptable delays, costs or sheer impossibilities, are no longer constraints for businesses in communicating either with employees working away from base or with other organisations, whether they be suppliers, customers, partners or even rivals.

What will the organisation of tomorrow look like?

We hesitate to give a prescriptive model of the organisation of tomorrow since individual businesses will embrace the concepts associated with the virtual organisation at a pace and to an extent suitable to them. Organisations will thus become virtual in different degrees: while a service- or information-based company may feel confident about conducting its business in cyberspace, manufacturing organisations will still produce physical goods for actual delivery, even if the intellectual effort involved in producing the product (an effort which may have a value greater than that of the physical content) is itself a 'virtual' activity.

There are, however, some trends which have emerged over the last 10 years or so which do give some strong indications as to how organisations will develop:

- Organisational structures will be horizontal rather than hierarchical; transient rather than static.
- There will be more teamworking, particularly of a cross-functional, cross-organisational nature.
- Individuals will be more mobile both within and between organisations.
- There will be a greater use of teleworking and other forms of flexible working, made possible by advances in computing and telecommunications.
- There will be greater cooperation between companies to win access to new markets.
- Businesses will concentrate on what they are best at, and outsource the rest.
- Organisations will become skilled at learning and adapting, to sustain a competitive advantage.

In Thursday's and Saturday's chapters, we will consider the organisational model of the future in more detail and give some pointers on how an organisation might seek to determine its own evolution.

When will this change take place?

Five or ten more years will see the convergence of factors which could lead to the emergence of truly virtual organisations. Even today, however:

- technology has advanced to the point where such organisations are already feasible
- trends such as those listed above are already well developed and are becoming characteristics of *virtuality*
- issues prompted by the organisational downsizings of the 1980s and 1990s, such as concerns about the destruction of the psychological contract and the loss of employee loyalty, are beginning to be addressed
- younger managers who have grown up in the age of personal computing are now beginning to find themselves in positions of influence.

While the majority of us may not be greatly affected over the next few years, some of us will find ourselves working in new ways. Indeed, many may find themselves forced to alter their working patterns by organisations wishing to take advantage of the flexibility and cost-effectiveness that the virtual organisation is bringing in. There are, however, many questions to address and many problems to be solved before the transformation to virtual organisations can take place, and these centre more on the willingness of society, organisations and individuals to embrace the changes needed, than on the capability of technology to deliver.

Why is it happening?

There are several reasons for the trend towards virtuality:

- the need to respond rapidly to change and to maximise the speed to market of new products
- the pace of change in markets and technology, which is such that one organisation cannot keep up with it alone
- the increasing sophistication of consumers, who are demanding quality, choice and value for money

- the convergence of information technologies which allow work to be done by fewer people, more productively and in more flexible ways
- the growth in importance of the individual who values loyalty to a profession above loyalty to one organisation, and who values their private and working lives equally
- the disappearance of the job for life and of progress up the career ladder
- the trend towards greater mobility between, and greater flexibility within, jobs

- the increased costs and problems involved in travelling from A to B
- the shift from a manufacturing-based to an information-based economy, where the value of the intellectual content of a product is greater than that of the physical content.

During the week, we shall discuss these trends in more detail.

What might slow it down?

We have identified three barriers to the development of the virtual organisation:

1 Inadequacies in the existing hardware and software infrastructure.
2 Organisational and management attitudes towards people and technology.
3 The reluctance of individuals to adopt a flexible approach to employment.

Inadequacies in the existing computing infrastructure
Although great strides have been made in computing capability, there are challenges still remaining:

- The present man–machine interface is now old-fashioned (decades ago, keyboards were designed in a way that slows typists down, screens use pre-war technology, and even the mouse is now 20 years old).
- There is a need to access information by displaying it graphically so that managers can spot problems quickly without having to read through reams of text.

- Research has yet to address how, in 5–10 years' time, we will harness the computer literacy of the next generation, who will use technology of awesome power compared to the machines of today.
- There is a very real danger that national governments may fail to invest sufficiently or quickly enough in modern communications. Data exchange is increasingly achieved by fibre optic and satellite links, some privately and some publicly funded. Due to a reluctance so far on the part of governments to fund investment, many communications links – primarily those used by what is referred to as the *Internet*, (see Tuesday's chapter) – are too slow and incapable of supporting the widespread shift towards electronic working that the concept of the virtual organisation proposes.

Managers' attitudes towards people and technology
Most organisations still retain a *command and control* structure. Managers fear that flexible work arrangements will result in chaos, with employees not being available when needed or not doing the work they were employed to do. Despite increasing empowerment, there remains a lack of trust about anybody or anything which cannot be seen. Many managers rely on *face time* (the amount of time spent at the office) to measure performance, and this leads to employees putting in long hours at their desk regardless of the level of effectiveness of the work done. New management techniques for managing remote workers therefore need to be devised which will centre on effective communication and work-organisation skills.

Managers may not have sufficient understanding of technology and the potential it offers. Those who have had bad experiences with IT projects in the past will be sceptical of the benefits of communications technologies.

The reluctance of individuals to be more flexible
Most people, until recently, were used to secure, long-term employment which supported their family and mortgage, and as a result it is difficult for individuals to revolutionise their way of life and turn with confidence to the concept of *contract working*. Organisations therefore need to help employees to prepare for a world where no-one is guaranteed a job for life, where people need to manage their own careers, and where relationships with co-workers will be less personal and more fluid. They need to help them to develop a range of transferable skills such as those associated with computer literacy, languages, teamworking and communication.

How will it affect the way I work?

You will no longer be confined to a 9-to-5 working day or a
particular place of work. You will not necessarily sit next to
or near the people you are managing or with whom you
are working: they could be at the other end of the building
or on the other side of the world. You will no longer have
one routine job but instead will collaborate on several
projects at once with different team members from varying
disciplines, and these arrangements will arise and then
dissolve according to the needs of your organisation. You
will have less job security, but you will be empowered and
trusted to work on your own initiative, and with
responsibility, according to guidelines rather than strict
rules. You will need to be self-motivated and to take charge
of your own career, continually updating your skills and
knowledge, not least in the area of technology.

What are the benefits?

The virtual organisation can lead to:

- distance being no object in the carrying out of work,
  meetings, collaborations or conferences
- a minimising of the effects of physical disasters such as
  fires, bomb attacks and earthquakes, or of other
  disruptive events, such as a rail strike, as business
  activities are no longer concentrated in one building or
  on one site
- an increased emphasis on the human side of work as
  the mechanical, repetitive, soul-destroying elements are
  stripped out

- significant productivity improvements
- a reduction in the costs of office floor space as various forms of flexible working are introduced
- environmental benefits as fewer people travel to and from work
- better quality for the customer.

We shall summarise further benefits of the virtual organisation on Saturday.

What are the dangers?

- As the division between work and home life becomes blurred, stress levels can rise.
- Staff can become socially isolated, lacking the stimulus of personal contact and feedback.
- If the employment relationship is not redesigned, the commitment of valuable knowledge (i.e. virtual) workers to the organisation will be low, and they will sell their skills to the highest bidder. The resulting high staff turnover will have an adverse effect on the success of the firm.

- Employees who are not core knowledge workers may be sidelined. Unless efforts are also made to train, involve and support those people inside the organisation whose work is still physical rather than virtual, and to care in a similar way for small contractors outside the organisation, the virtual organisation will lead to a divided society.

Why do I need to bother with virtuality?

Virtuality in organisations is already changing the way we do business, so it is important, sooner rather than later, to look at how your company can work without the traditional constraints of time, place or physical resources. It is important to be able to make informed judgements on the benefits and the problems virtuality is bringing, so that you can position your organisation correctly to deal with the pace of change and competition in markets. It is not enough to understand the capabilities of the new technologies: a re-evaluation of working practices, structures and management processes is also vital.

Summary

Today we have considered several meanings of the concept 'virtual organisation', looked at the impact of virtuality on organisations and individuals – today and in the future – and reviewed the benefits and dangers it brings. Over the rest of the week we shall develop further the ideas introduced in this chapter, focusing tomorrow on the trends towards virtuality in the evolving organisation.

The reinvention of organisations

Today we shall outline some of the changes which have taken place in the marketplace in the last three decades, and examine organisational responses to them. We shall look at how organisations are reinventing themselves by adopting new management processes and structures, and shall consider the effect on employees. These changes have significance for the virtual organisation: they are leading both organisations and employees to become more adaptable, which is, in turn, a preparation for the greater flexibility and agility which the virtual organisation will demand. The key issues include:

- changes in the marketplace
- the search for quality
- downsizing
- core competencies
- outsourcing
- business process re-engineering
- speed to market
- teamworking
- empowerment

Changes in the marketplace

The marketplace has changed in the last three decades from a state of stability and uniformity to one of volatility and variability. Consider the following developments:

- The world has shrunk due to cheaper travel, more efficient telecommunications, television bringing the world into your living room, and the connectivity of computer networks.
- Markets have become global, with consumer products of all kinds, such as Coca-Cola and McDonald's hamburgers, sold anywhere from New York to Moscow.
- Customers have become more demanding, wanting quality, choice, value for money, good service and fast delivery.

- There is fierce competition between firms, ease of entry into markets, and rapid product obsolescence.
- There has been an astonishing rate of technological change, such that no one organisation can keep pace with it.

Organisations have responded to trends such as these by shifting their market strategy from a focus on products to a focus on meeting customer needs, and to a search for competitiveness. Competitiveness derives from an organisation's capability to deliver better goods and services, more cheaply, more quickly and more consistently than the competition. Today we shall look at some of the techniques which organisations have used in pursuit of competitiveness.

The search for quality

For many, the search for better goods and services has meant a search for quality, and this has led to the following developmental sequence:

- *quality control* – putting things right after they have gone wrong
- *quality circles* – involving staff in putting things right and making them better
- *quality systems* – a focus on internal procedures to assure a certain level of performance and delivery
- *benchmarking* – looking outside the organisation to monitor the standards, targets and performance of market leaders
- *total quality management* – an all-embracing philosophy whereby the whole workforce uses a range of techniques and methods to achieve the goal of continuous improvement for the customer.

In many cases, the search for quality has concentrated on reducing costs.

Downsizing

With markets subject to rapid change, large organisations have proved to be unwieldy and slow to adapt. One of the earliest responses to the need to cut costs, speed up organisational processes and get closer to the customer was *delayering*. There has been a consistent trend towards reducing the number of staff and the number of management layers, although this is now beginning to slow. Such *downsizing* has made some organisations more profitable, more effective and more customer-focused, but in others it has led to corporate anorexia, with surviving staff overworked and feeling demotivated and insecure.

In some organisations, however, downsizing has been the result not of short-term cost-cutting exercises but of questioning the core business and deciding where to go in the future and how to get there.

Core competencies

The key to understanding how an organisation can reach a position of competitiveness is to analyse what it is that it does that is *better* than what others can do. The answers will lead to the identification of the organisation's *core competencies*. The concept of core competencies looks at the organisation not as a portfolio of products and services but as a system of activities, some of which are more critical than others. The process of identifying core competencies looks not necessarily at the end product only but also at the building blocks.

Core competencies cannot be dropped and picked up again at will: they take years to develop and nurture. There are four key stages:

1 *Identification.* Identifying the organisation's key activities is not a case of brainstorming lists of possibilities but more a question of asking:

   • How important is X as a customer benefit? Does it make a significant improvement to the end product for the customer?
   • Does X provide potential access to a range of applications and markets?
   • If we were to lose our strength in X, could we still safeguard our future competitiveness?
   • How difficult is it for others to imitate X and compete directly with us?

2 *Consensus.* The development and renewal of core competencies will involve resource and energy consumption. It is therefore important that senior management agrees on where the focus of activity should

be. This will involve an agreement on the very nature of the business itself, and an awareness of the implications of letting core competencies steer decisions and actions.

3 *Organisation.* Advocates of core competencies argue that the role of senior management is to identify, develop and organise around those key activities which are both unique and reinforceable and which are known to be difficult to imitate. Competencies will need constant strengthening and input, and to be managed in a way that delivers the best advantage they can offer.

4 *An external perspective.* Markets continue to change and evolve, requiring modifications and improvements. There is a danger of concentrating too much within the four walls of the organisation. Not everything you need will be found on the inside, and the cost of developing and launching new products in new markets continues to escalate. Some organisations are looking outside, even to competitors, to form partnerships and alliances of mutual benefit. Organising around core competencies means encouraging people to keep up-to-date by networking with peers in other, rival organisations. In some cases, this can go beyond informal contacts to the formation of a collaborative venture for a specific purpose or project to which each partner brings their core competencies. We shall look more at partnerships and collaboration on Thursday.

Outsourcing

One result of identifying core competencies is the opportunity to use outsourcing to work with carefully selected outside partners who can add value to the functioning of your organisation. This was summed up by Tom Peters when he said, 'Do what you do best and outsource the rest.' Traditional outsourcing targets have been those areas which make up the support, administration and internal servicing of the organisation. These areas do not add special value to your products and services, but they are nonetheless fundamental to running the organisation. Such areas are not difficult to identify, and examples include catering, transport, printing, advertising, and security. More recently, some organisations have expanded the boundaries of outsourcing and contracted out IT services, public relations and even accounting, training and information processing.

The key is to identify what is vital to the future of the business; it is crucial, therefore, to understand the full scope of the activity under consideration. How far, for example, does the accounting function play a much wider role than that of financial management and analysis? How far does training play a role in the developmental learning of the organisation? How much of information processing is down to data-sorting, and how much is it integrated into strategic decision-making? If managers are not careful, outsourcing can result in a reduction in an organisation's robustness, ability to integrate functions and processes, and capacity to learn and develop.

Organisations are quick to seize on the greater financial flexibility brought about by reducing overheads, and to want to benefit from the efficiencies created by contracting out activities to specialist agencies, but slimmer does not necessarily mean fitter. Functions and departments tend to be subject to outsourcing because they comprise identifiable chunks, but in the drive for flexibility and cost-savings, outsourcing is prone to becoming an end in itself.

If you are going to outsource, there are nine golden rules:

1 Analyse your current strengths and weaknesses.
2 Understand the full scope of each function or department.
3 Pay attention to people's motivation and security.
4 Find out what other organisations are doing.
5 Outsource the 'doing' of an activity, not the responsibility for it.
6 Choose a partner agency with great care.
7 Look before you leap with a test period.
8 Don't outsource strategic, customer or financial management.
9 Repeat step 3.

Business process re-engineering (BPR)

Unlike outsourcing, the main focus of *business process re-engineering* (BPR) is on those very processes, activities and cross-functional links whose value may not be perceived when the organisation is viewed functionally or hierarchically. The objective of BPR is to look for dramatic improvements in quality, customer service and costs by concentrating on processes rather than on general functions and individual tasks. It has proved to be a popular approach in the 1990s, partly due to the spectacular gains in performance, productivity and profitability made by companies such as Ford, Rank Xerox and Kodak. There has been much misunderstanding, however, about what is involved and what can be achieved.

BPR can have a revolutionary impact on the organisation, and its proponents argue, indeed, that it *must* create radical changes if a quantum leap in performance is to be achieved. Like total quality management (TQM), BPR requires extensive commitment to problem-solving and teamworking. Unlike TQM, however, its essence lies in discontinuous thinking and in getting away from old assumptions and routine thinking. At the risk of oversimplification, the basic steps of BPR are as follows:

1 What exactly is to be re-engineered? Make sure objectives are agreed, realistic and measurable.
2 Analyse first those processes that have caused customer dissatisfaction.
3 Decide whether you are targeting improvements to costs, time or quality of output.
4 Adopt performance indicators against which performance improvements can be measured.
5 Be prepared to allow time for process analysis.

The drive towards re-engineering process efficiency and effectiveness stems from an awareness that flexible, variable processes can have flexible, variable outcomes, or products. It is also a recognition that customers want things not only of the best quality and at the lowest cost, but also as fast as possible.

Speed to market

If the production lines of the past were accompanied by warehouses of goods that had no sell-by date, the production process of today has assimilated the demands of a diverse and changing market, characterised by swift obsolescence and the requirement for more timely delivery. *Just-in-time manufacturing* uses IT to link production with logistics to reduce stock-holdings and enable more efficient distribution. Manufacturing systems can convert a product from a computer design to a solid replica in days rather than weeks or months. New techniques such as *lean production, simultaneous engineering* and *fast-track development* use IT to allow producers to gain a fleeting competitive edge in the market.

As product life-cycles diminish, manufacturers must continuously learn about the performance and life-time of their products when they are with the customer, as well as ensuring shorter development times. Now, it is not only marketers but also producers who must get closer to the customer in relationships that involve working together, almost as part of a team.

Teamworking

A team is a group of people who share common objectives, who need to work together to achieve them and for which they hold themselves mutually accountable. There are three identifiable trends in the use of teambuilding:

1 It is increasing rapidly. A recent Industrial Society survey reported that 86% of its respondents had stated that their organisation has invested significantly more in teambuilding over the past two to three years, and that this trend is set to continue.
2 Fewer layers in organisational structures make it possible for cross-functional teams to be formed which cut across previous rigid functional barriers.
3 As teams take on more skills and more responsibility, they become *self-directing*, with the role of the manager changing to one of facilitator or coach.

Self-directed teams
Self-directed teams have the following characteristics:

- Shared leadership. A member will be a leader at certain times and a participant at other times.

- Team members are interdependent. They are capable both of working independently when they need to and also of collaborating with, or relying on, others to complete a task.
- Everyone feels that they count. Every team member must have the opportunity to negotiate their roles and clarify their relationships with one another.
- Team members have a sense of ownership. The more employees understand and value the team goal, the more effective the team will be. Everybody must be free to learn and contribute.
- Everyone has clearly defined roles. This means that each team member knows what is expected of them and who to go to with problems and concerns.
- There is a team facilitator. One member should have underlying responsibility for setting the team's direction and knowing where to go outside the group to solve problems.

Empowerment

As a result of delayering, teambuilding and total quality management programmes, some companies have made serious efforts to develop and maintain *empowerment*. The reasons for this are two-fold: a wish to provide a better service for customers and a need to harness the creativity of all employees to heighten a firm's competitiveness. Empowerment involves giving people greater responsibility and devolving decision-making. It should be viewed not as a technique but more as a form of organisational culture which relies for its success or failure on the attitudes and behaviour of managers and employees. For empowerment to flourish, a style of management is required which is based on mutual respect, open communication, supportive guidance and freedom from blame. The manager becomes a leader or facilitator rather than a supervisor, developing and maintaining conditions which will allow others to care about and accept responsibility for obtaining results.

The skills required for empowerment include:

- providing information and sharing it with all those who need it to do their job
- facilitating communication so that everyone is included in the picture
- coaching and counselling to enable individual and organisational development
- maintaining self-esteem by developing mutual respect and giving responsibility
- setting goals which are challenging, realistic and mutually agreed

- facilitating business processes by involving those who do the job
- providing the resources, tools and responsibility to do the job.

The creation of an empowered environment takes time. Line managers have to be empowered by their superiors before they in turn can empower others. Employees may be reluctant to accept responsibility and involvement, particularly if they see it as just a delegation of blame when things go wrong.

Implications of the new ways of managing

- The organisation understands what it is best at.
- Companies are more ready to look outside and collaborate with other firms for mutual advantage.
- Businesses place a premium on quality goods and services, and on customer satisfaction.
- Individuals are more and more used to working in teams.
- Employees are happier to take responsibility and work on their own.

Summary

Today, we have looked at some management foundations of the virtual organisation. Tomorrow we shall go on to look at another key enabling factor: telecommunications technologies.

The communications revolution

In the mid-1990s, the convergence of formerly separate technologies has enabled organisations to be more flexible both in the way they are structured and in the way they carry out their work. In some aspects, the pace of technological change has outstripped the ability of businesses to keep up. Today we shall look at the developments which have improved intra- and inter-organisational communications and focus on the advantages to business. We shall look at:

- the dimensions of technological change
- telecommunication lines
- the Internet
- video-conferencing
- groupware
- the Intranet
- the telephone
- computer integrated telephony

The dimensions of technological change

Consider the following trends:

- *Power:* microchips are doubling in performance every 18 months.
- *Cost:* computer prices drop by approximately 30% every year.
- *Miniaturisation:* an ever-increasing amount of information can be processed and stored on one microchip.

- *Volume:* more than 12 million computers have been sold in the UK since 1990. There are also 4 million mobile-phone users and 2 million fax machines. There are over 40 million e-mail addresses world-wide.
- *Downsizing:* there is a move away from mainframe-based systems with central processing towards PC networks that distribute data across organisations.
- *Connectivity:* modems are increasingly sold as standard, and computers are increasingly being connected to local and national networks.
- *Digitalisation:* national and international telecommunications networks are switching to digital to improve efficiency, speed and quality of transmission.

Today we shall concentrate on the convergence of computing and telecommunications, and on how this is blurring the differences between internal and external communications and enabling effective networking across time and space. Later on, we shall look at applications which are removing the need for travelling – for 'being there' – but first we look at the developments in telecommunication lines which enable such applications to work.

Telecommunication lines

To connect one computer to another requires a *link*.
Internally, this is usually done through special cabling to
specific points on a *local area network* (LAN), and in the near
future, the installation of *structured cabling* will provide
such internal networks with the flexibility to move
equipment around without the intervention of specialist
staff. Externally, it can be done by *telephone lines* running
through the local exchange into the national and
international networks. While these normal telephone lines
have functioned adequately for transporting data or text,
the lines themselves are too limiting for the effective
carriage and delivery of graphics, images and video: i.e.
they do not have enough *bandwidth* capacity. A simple
colour image, for example, can take several minutes to send
over standard telephone lines; video would probably jam
up the lines and never even get there!

These problems can be overcome by the use of a *leased* (kilostream or megastream) *line* direct to a specific location. This gives greater bandwidth, but it can also prove expensive. Now, however, two communication technologies are developing the capability of greater quality and speed of delivery for the PC user at a lower cost: fibre optics and ISDN.

Fibre optics
Optical-fibre cables, which are tiny strands of pure glass, carry messages as pulses of light. The copper wires of the old network are adequate for voice signals but are subject to interference and lack the broad bandwidth necessary for image, graphics and video. Optical-fibres, on the other hand, have almost unlimited bandwidth, are practically immune to interference and are now installed at major telecommunication junction points and exchanges in the UK. It is estimated that optical-fibre links now carry more than 90% of UK telecommunications and 65% of international connections. Unfortunately, in many cases, the call or signal carried will still run into the old copper cables between the exchange and home or work, and there, grind to a halt.

ISDN
ISDN stands for Integrated Services Digital Network and can be installed by major telecommunications companies to furnish the final link from the main network to the home or office. ISDN relies on *digital* as opposed to *analogue* networks, and can replace the need for both leased lines for transmission and modems to encode the data to be sent. Let us look in detail at the transmission of data.

Data Transmission

The modem takes the digital information output from the PC and converts it into an analogue format for sending to the local exchange. Most local exchanges in the UK are now digital, so the information is usually converted back into digital format for sending down the main digital networks in the UK. It then reaches the local exchange at the penultimate junction in its destination, and there the information is reconverted back into analogue to go the final distance to the home or workplace. The modem at the receiver's end then reconverts the information back to digital so that it can be understood and read on the PC. The only part of this network that is still analogue is the part that links the home or office to the local exchange. However, ISDN can now complete the digital link by transforming the line between the home and the exchange so as to exploit the capability of the PC for the transfer of text, image, video, fax or telephone messages either separately or at the same time.

ISDN provides the secure and effective transmission of voice and non-voice data on a single network, and in addition:

- it can handle *multi media*
- it can be up to 50 times faster than conventional telephone lines for text transfer
- it facilitates a higher level of quality in electronic delivery, since digital is less susceptible than analogue to interference
- it allows for dial-up: instead of leasing the line, you only pay when you use it. Calls are at the same rate as for the standard network, but they consume less time and therefore less money
- it enables flexibility: ISDN allows organisations to build their own private virtual networks because communications between remote locations are now secure as well as powerful.

If ISDN can bring broad bandwidth and digital capability
to the home or office, how much does it cost?

ISDN costs
At the time of writing, an ISDN line can be installed for
about £400, the annual rental is around £330, and then there
are the usage charges not dissimilar to telephone charges.
Cost are likely to drop, not rise. This arrangement is called
ISDN2, and it provides two channels with digital capability.

British Telecom (BT) can install an ISDN line with 2, 6, 15 or
30 channels (see table), and other telecommunications
companies offer similar services at alternative prices.

BT charges for ISDN at 1996 approximate £ prices

	Installation	Rental	Adaptor/ Router	Usage
ISDN2	400	250	A: 650	Standard
ISDN6	600	720	R: 3,500	rates, but
ISDN15	1,500	1,800	R: 4,500	less
ISDN30	3,000	3,600	R: 4,500+	time.

Your PC will need an *adaptor*; or, if you wish to network access to
ISDN from a number of PCs, you will need a black box called a *router*.

The number of channels needed will depend on the type,
amount and speed of transmission required. Two will be
sufficient for a dedicated live video-link and much more
besides. However, the more applications, the more
simultaneous usage you intend and the more varied the data
transfer you require, the more channels you will need.

The prices in the table may look expensive, but weigh these
costs against alternative costs which organisations are
already paying, for example:

- the cost of transporting people to and from work or meetings away from the workplace
- the cost of supporting workers at the workplace
- the cost of opportunities and time lost in sending information through traditional channels.

Case study: Laura Ashley

Laura Ashley is one of the UK's major fashion and home furnishings retailers, with a presence in the USA, continental Europe, the Far East and Australia. The company had decided to explore an opportunity to gain competitive advantage through more efficient use of its *electronic point of sale* (EPOS) systems by using ISDN2 to link its in-store network to an automatic credit-card validation system and to head office, so that store PCs can be polled each day after the store is closed.

With the introduction of ISDN, high-speed credit-card transactions have reduced in-store queues, decreased the incidence of fraud and improved customer service. ISDN also allows the information on daily stock transactions to be collated and delivered quickly and reliably so as to provide a better – and faster – picture of the company's trading position.

Source: British Telecom Commstore on the World Wide Web.

ATM

ATM, or Asynchronous Transfer Mode, was originally developed to cope with the large quantity of data transmitted through local area networks. It is now being developed into an advanced form of high-speed telecommunications network which uses a new switching technology potentially capable of handling all types of telecommunications traffic across *wide area networks* (WANs) or to remote locations. At the time of writing, ATM remains a network for the future. Its use is still limited because of its high price, and it is not yet known when it will be cheap enough to take advantage of. But as ATM's development continues and more applications become available on it, its price will increasingly be assessed against the more time-honoured methods of transporting information and people.

The Internet

The Internet is a world-wide network of computer networks connected to each other by telecommunications links, and is made up of an ever-growing number of organisations and individuals who have decided to make information available in a giant, interconnected, open system. It has been estimated (using the logic that only statistics can afford) that if the current (1996) rate of connect-ups continues, then everyone on the planet will be connected up by the year 2005! It is asserted that the Internet will offer a new viable medium for the conduct of business transactions: a cyberspace world mirroring the real one but where time and place are irrelevant.

Although the use of the Internet does not require ISDN, the latter will enable far greater exploitation of the Internet as it offers a wide menu of information from multimedia mixes of video, graphics and sound to straight text. This mix requires a greater capacity than the old local analogue wiring from junction to home can supply.

There are currently three principal functions available on the Internet: communication (e-mail), information-gathering and marketing.

E-mail

E-mail (electronic mail) enables the transmission and receipt of messages and documents using PCs as letter boxes and telecommunication lines as postal services. The 'letter' is sent to, and sits in, a 'mail-box', for the recipient to receive or access. It stays there until disposed of. E-mail brings a number of benefits:

- Like a fax, it can be sent at a time convenient to the sender and read at a time convenient to the receiver. This is particularly useful when the correspondents are in different time zones or merely working at different times of the day, or where the recipient would not want interrupting.
- Like a fax or letter, it can handle not only text but also graphics.
- Like a fax but unlike a phone call, messages can be relayed one-to-one or one-to-many, with only one copy of the original.
- The cost of transmission is much cheaper than phone or fax and is not dependent on the distance the message has to travel.
- It cuts down on the use of paper (unlike fax) and increases the flexibility of the communication process (unlike a traditional telephone account).
- E-mail users do not have to be at home or at their desk to read their messages: all they need to do is dial into their mail box. An e-mail address, like a mobile phone or answer-phone, means that you are not tied to a particular place or time like a traditional postal address or telephone account.

Information-gathering

Although thousands of interconnected computers seem to offer an unprecedented opportunity for ensuring the delivery of information on demand, information-gathering can be hampered by the sheer volume of information and navigation problems. But as the Internet turns into the *information superhighway* and more organisations become connected, the quality of information is improving and search mechanisms are becoming more effective.

Marketing

The marketing potential of the Internet is one of the main attractions for businesses seeking to explore the potential of a world-wide market through the *World Wide Web* (WWW), a software program which cross-references, links and retrieves data from computers around the world in seamless moves, using a *hypertext* system. Hypertext allows you to move from one document to another and one computer to another using a mouse to click on highlighted terms or graphics. On the WWW, this facility creates an impressive version of what cyberspace can be.

Marketing on the Internet is establishing its own protocols and rules of acceptance, and, as on the billboards, newspapers and TV, there is good and there is bad marketing. One of the essential factors distinguishing the Internet from these other media is *interactivity*. The Internet is not just about watching and reading, it's about making your site interesting so that people will want to return to it. As an advertiser on the WWW, you can't target your customers directly, but they can send requests – and complaints – direct to you through e-mail.

At the time of writing, banks are working with software houses to find foolproof, unbreakable ways of ensuring secure, confidential payments on the Internet. In due course – and sooner rather than later – they will offer secure methods for organisations and individuals to try.

For more information about The Internet, see *Understanding Business on the Internet* in this series.

Video-conferencing

Video-conference links allow groups of people in remote locations to see as well as hear each other via a live video connection. The connection is created by a telecommunications link (ISDN) and enables people to conduct live 'meetings' in cyberspace. In this way it can create a shared work environment for individuals separated by time and distance.

Video-conferencing units have been around for some time but have been slow to be adopted probably because business has failed to recognise any benefit or value for the cost of outlay. Now, however, with video-conference costs dropping and ISDN making distance-working a realistic

'CYBERSPACE'

alternative to physical travel, the benefits of investing in new technology have to be weighed against the costs of physically 'being there'.

One obstacle to the more widespread use of video-conferencing is that it appears not only fantastical but rather 'big-brotherish'. On the other hand, people who have tried it get more of a feeling of 'being there' than with the telephone: people get to talk face-to-face.

Case study: Lloyds Bank plc

The UK retail banking arm of Lloyds Bank recognised a need for frequent meetings between the commercial managers based in Bristol, and the IT specialists – developing new applications – based in London. Because of continuing high travel costs, the business case was made for video-conferencing.

Within nine months of implementation, there had been a 20% reduction in the spend on rail travel, in addition to the time saved. After a while, it was found that people come better

---

prepared for a video-conference, and that such meetings are concluded quicker than those with a physical location. As people become more used to video-conferencing, it is replacing the more traditional methods of working, especially in planning marketing campaigns, press conferences and even recruitment.

Source: British Telecom, Commstore on the World Wide Web.

Groupware

Just as ISDN enables video-conference links to provide a shared work environment mirroring the real world, so it can also enable *groupware* to provide the common platform for remote individuals to share information. Groupware achieves this by:

- allowing people in appropriate groups special access to bulletin boards on the network, which allows dialogues on-screen
- organising information for easy collection and distribution
- combining information from different sources into new documents.

The purpose of groupware is to get information *direct* to those who need it rather than making them *fetch* it – for example, from a database. With a database, they might not know it is there unless warned. With groupware, on the other hand, the information is signalled to you. For work at whatever stage and of whatever origin, this can speed up the internal distribution of information.

Groupware enables the organisation to restructure teams across physical boundaries without physically relocating the employee. One application of groupware, Lotus Notes, is already in use in thousands of organisations. Lotus Notes can act both as a secretary, recording everything at a meeting, and as a project monitor recording schedules and keeping participants up-to-date with overall progress. Used in conjunction with video-conferencing, groupware can create live teams, and facilitate meetings and decision-making across time and space.

The Intranet

The *Intranet* is another example of growing the internal network externally, not by Lotus Notes groupware, but by basing the network on World Wide Web technology. Intranets share the same software, network technology and computer language as the Internet. However, while the Internet is a global network open to all, Intranets exist only within organisations, fenced off from external communications by 'firewalls'. The organisation's employees can communicate safely internally and look outside at the Internet at large, but anyone outside cannot get in. The result is a new kind of groupware which allows the organisation to take advantage of Web technology and blurs, but safeguards, the distinction between internal and external communications. It also shares the Internet's appeal of enabling anyone to become a multimedia publisher without any of the costs of traditional publication or distribution: one copy of a document on the organisation's Intranet server is enough for *all* employees to read or download.

The telephone

Whatever happens with new technology, the humble telephone still remains at the core of business communication. But it is not so humble any more. In the 1970s, it was said that half of Europe was waiting for a line to be installed while the other half was waiting to obtain a dialling tone. Let us look at just some of the developments since.

- Memory storage for regularly used numbers.
- Loud speakers to project messages beyond the receiver.
- A call-back number to see who called when you were out.
- Experimental centralised answerphone services to do away with a personal machine.
- A caller-display which displays the number of the person calling so you can decide whether to pick up the call, leave it for your answer-machine or voice-mail or just not bother.
- Call waiting, which lets you know if someone else is trying to get through when you are already on the phone.
- Three-way calling – to talk to two other numbers either together or one at a time.
- Voice-mail which pages you to dial in to see who called you.
- Message relays to divert calls to another number.
- Mobile phones, with or without voice-mail, which mean that you can be anywhere at any time and still keep in touch.

By integrating with the computer, the telephone can help managers regain control over a device which has long dominated time management and interrupted planning schedules. By integrating with the organisation's customer database, the telephone can also offer a quicker response to the customer.

Computer integrated telephony (CIT)

Computer integrated telephony (CIT) uses a process called *calling line identification* (CLI). When customers call, CLI – linked to the organisation's customer database – identifies where they are calling from and 'pops up' the customer account on the receiver's computer screen before the receiver picks up the phone. (One caveat is that CLI picks up the number from which the call is dialled, and if that number is not matched to the database – for example, if the customer calls from a call box – then CLI will not work.) While some companies are exploring CIT, others are going further to cut out human intervention altogether: *voice response systems* can put the customer directly in contact with the database, using touch-tone input, and deliver voice-processed information in return.

Summary

IT has now made such progress in bringing together technologies for business solutions that it now has to wait for business to catch up. For some, exploring new technological potential may require a leap of faith: there probably still remain many scars from the damaging hype of the past, and businesses will need to see the cost benefits before taking the plunge. Younger managers, trained on databases and the Internet, will not need that leap of faith, however.

Cheaper alternatives to yesterday's methods are now being found. Converging technologies have brought about a new balance between 'I' (information) and 'T' (technology), and that balance can change the way we organise and carry out our work. We look at these tomorrow.

The virtual workplace

Today we examine how the workplace is becoming more mobile and flexible, focusing on innovations in the use of office space. These changes are being brought about by the need for organisations to speed up response times, improve flexibility and cut costs, and by the use of telecommunications technologies which allow people to do more of their work remotely. We shall consider:

- teleworking
- telecentres
- mobile working
- hot-desking
- hotelling
- virtual teams
- the computer-generated virtual office
- the benefits and problems of the virtual office

Teleworking

Teleworking involves carrying out work at a location remote from the workplace (usually, but not necessarily, at home) and communicating with the employer through the use of computer and telecommunications equipment. Such equipment allows the worker to connect to common organisational databases and groupware, and to correspond with their manager via e-mail. It can also enable communications traffic in the reverse direction by allowing home-based staff to share in the handling of customer service calls which are routed to them by an automatic call distributor, the caller unaware that they are talking to an agent working in their own home rather than in a central office.

Research published at Newcastle University in 1995 put the use of teleworking at less than 1 worker in 100. A recent survey by Dataquest found, however, that some 50% of companies in the UK now have remotely located workers, and another study, published by the Institute of Management and Manpower, suggests that managers expect the use of teleworking to grow in the next 10 years. There is certainly evidence to show that organisations are becoming increasingly interested in various forms of teleworking, and that employees too are now more ready to accept homeworking as the importance of 'owning' physical space in the office decreases and improvements in technology mean that remote workers are less isolated than in the past.

Although some companies employ people who work at home permanently, successful schemes show that a mix of teleworking and time at the office for briefing and social interaction is a more practical combination. Such an arrangement also makes it easier for managers to monitor and motivate employees whom they no longer see face-to-face every day.

At the moment, there is a tendency to appraise teleworkers by measuring their level of output. As teleworking spreads, however, to a wider range of jobs and workers, managers must move away from measuring merely the quantity of work to take a more strategic view of teleworking and develop ways of assessing quality, determining success by the question: is this contributing towards better customer service?

Checklist for introducing teleworking

1 Carry out a feasibility study. Include a cost–benefit analysis in the study, taking into account productivity, communication and training costs, administrative support requirements and office space.
2 Decide on the basis on which you will introduce teleworking. Will it be organisation-wide or on a departmental or functional basis? Decide which individual jobs are suitable for teleworking.
3 Conduct a pilot study and evaluate the results.
4 Ensure that teleworkers have the necessary personal qualities and skills. These include maturity, trustworthiness, self-sufficiency, self-discipline, good time management, communications skills and a knowledge of how to use the hardware and software provided. Training and retraining may be needed – do not underestimate their importance.

5 Put the right communications structures in place.
People must have the right tools to do the job required.
Hardware and software should be compatible with the
equipment used elsewhere in the organisation, have the
same maintenance and insurance cover, be
ergonomically sound and be kept up-to-date.
6 Draw up a contract. Additional clauses to a standard
employment contract should cover health and safety, working
hours, reporting procedures and equipment responsibilities.
7 Provide facilities for teleworkers on office days. (See the
section on hot-desking later on today.)
8 Set up support systems for teleworkers. Try to create a
sense of belonging. Ensure that teleworkers receive the
same newsletters, offers of training and details of social
events as other employees.

9 Set up effective management systems. Ensure that
there is regular, informal contact between the employee
and the manager to discuss any problems and to check
progress. Include teleworkers in staff appraisal and
development systems.

Telecentres

It is expensive to equip large numbers of homes with all the equipment which an employee might need and which is common in most offices. Furthermore, not all homes can provide the space and peace necessary for work, and some people prefer to maintain a dividing line between home and work. In such situations, *telecentres* or *telecottages* can be the answer, replacing long journeys to work and compensating for a lack of facilities at home. These centres, which offer shared multimedia facilities, are either owned by one organisation providing their employees with a local work environment, or are independent and are used by a range of employers.

Case study: United Airlines

In Summer 1995, United Airlines opened three *neighbourhood satellite offices* (NSOs) near Los Angeles, San Francisco and Chicago. These NSOs use a form of automated call distribution developed by AT&T. This allows a customer enquiry from anywhere in North America to be automatically routed through its network to the first available agent in any of the offices.

United Airlines' new approach has had three benefits.

1 Employees who formerly had long journeys to work in the central reservation centres at the airports in the big cities have cut their commuting time drastically. This has given them more time to spend with their families or on leisure and charitable activities, or simply to relax.
2 The company now has a workforce which is more energetic and self-motivated.

> 3 The communities where the NSOs are located benefit from
>   the new jobs in their towns.
>
> *Source:* 'For your information column', 'United Airlines New
> Telecommuting Program Soars' by Gillian Flynn, copyright
> February 1996. Used with the permission of *Personnel Journal*,
> ACC Communications Inc., Costa Mesa, California; all rights
> reserved.

Mobile working

Mobile or nomadic workers, such as salespeople,
consultants or service technicians, need the tools to access
the same information as that available to desk-bound
workers. This requires an interchangeable use of mobile
telephony, fax and e-mail for communicating, and remote
access to groupware or Internet software to facilitate the
efficient sharing and transfer of information. These tools
enable the mobile worker to operate efficiently at home, in
an office, on the road or in a hotel. As with home-based
teleworkers, it is not just a question of supplying employees
with hardware and software: the costs of training,
maintenance of equipment and communications line
charges, for example, must also be built in. Mobile working
can bring tangible benefits, however, such as improved
productivity and better customer service. For example,
salespeople who win orders can now process them
themselves on the spot (providing they are empowered to
negotiate and close deals) rather than having to return to
head office and wait for a clerk to handle them.

Hot-desking

Most conventional offices are only full for a fraction of the time they are open because of sickness or holidays, or because some members of staff spend a significant part of their time on customers' premises. Since this arrangement means a waste of space and other resources, some organisations are turning to *hot-desking*. This is defined as the removal of permanent, individual desks for some or all employees. Instead, staff are allocated a *workstation* when they arrive at the office, and from there they can access their own e-mail and computer network files. In this system, personal space is restricted to drawers in filing cabinets or the use of a locker, but general space is made available for group or team activities. Usually, those who work full-time at base are given their own desks, but in some companies which operate hot-desking, *all* employees may be subject to the arrangement.

Those organisations which have introduced hot-desking have used this opportunity not only to create a more cost-efficient way of working but also to give offices a much higher standard of service and equipment. Such changes need a cautious approach, however, as the loss of personal territory can upset some employees. One answer is to provide an airport-style 'club' lounge where people can meet, collect mail and take part in leisure and social activities.

Checklist for introducing hot-desking

1   Assess the patterns of office use. Evaluate all working processes and activities, functional requirements and demands, and social and interactive needs, as well as occupancy patterns.

---

2 Conduct staff attitude surveys. Gather opinions on the importance of the various forms of workspace currently offered.

3 Reduce workstations to a number consistent with the usual maximum number of people in the office at any one time.

4 Cater for different needs, by providing:

- areas for quiet concentration
- group areas for meetings, training and team collaboration
- busy areas for telephoning
- extensively fitted workstations for a full mix of work
- drop-in areas with small worktop spaces
- resident space.

5 Devise a booking system. This should allow staff to:

- check availability
- reserve space
- modify reservations
- confirm or cancel.

6 Ensure that itinerants have a portable telephone extension so that their calls are routed to them at whichever desk they are sitting.

7 Provide storage space such as lockers or filing cabinets.

8 Consider the psychological issues. Some employees may regret the loss of their own office desk and space because it leaves them feeling insecure and disenfranchised.

9 Monitor the efficiency and effectiveness of the hot-desking facilities. An analysis of management information supplied by the booking system can help to anticipate any changes needed.

Hotelling

Hotelling extends the concept of hot-desking. Some employees, such as salespeople and consultants, spend most of their time with customers rather than at their employer's premises. They therefore rely on their clients to provide a desk and stay in contact with colleagues through telecommunication and computer links. When they need to work at base, they are allocated a desk on the hot-desk principle described above.

Case study: The Virtual Office

The Virtual Office is a company that provides a service enabling other companies to operate wherever they choose but always to be contactable on one central telephone number. This service also makes it possible to have a Central London presence without the expense of a permanent office.

Because every client that uses The Virtual Office is given their own 'phone number, calls are answered in the company name. The receptionist uses a specially designed CIT database so that information about the individual client is displayed on their screen as the call arrives. The call is then transferred to where the business operates – which could be at the other end of the country, on a mobile telephone or even overseas.

Other services offered include a *fax box* and a *pop-up PA*. A fax box is a computerised disk that stores the information sent by fax. This enables faxes to be transferred to any other fax machine using the tone keys found on most telephones, so that a businessperson can be anywhere in the world and still be able to receive faxes sent to their London fax number. A pop-up PA is a part-time personal assistant who is available full-time but to whom the client does not pay a full-time salary. This PA will deal with telephone calls, make appointments, write letters and the like.

The Virtual Office is supported by the full range of office facilities: advanced telephone, voice-mail and database systems; secretarial and postal services; photocopiers; and office space. Clients can make use of the company's premises when they visit London. *Touchdown desks* are available for short visits, and rooms can be booked for meetings. This is how it works.

Tom, who owns a small business in Leeds, wants a London office with full support, but without taking on the overheads. He spends a lot of time travelling, so back-up support is most important. Tom decides to become a client of The Virtual Office. He is given his own 0171 business telephone number, and the calls are redirected to any telephone number he chooses; usually, this is his home number, but sometimes it is his mobile, or it could even be a customer's number. He leaves instructions as to where he can be contacted with The Virtual Office, and as he does so, he takes the opportunity to have a chat with the people in the office: it can often be lonely working on your own. His calls are answered for him by the receptionist using the name of his company and in the manner he prefers.

She then tries to transfer the call. If the phone is busy or not answered, then she invites the caller to leave a voice-mail message or to be put through to his pop-up PA, Mary, who works at home in Luton and has Tom's electronic diary.

Tom uses the address in Piccadilly on all his business stationery. His mail is collected each day at The Virtual Office and, according to his standing instructions, forwarded to him or to Mary who decides how to deal with it. Occasionally, Tom's work brings him to London. He meets his clients at The Virtual Office where he books a room for the day. This also gives him another opportunity to meet the staff and chat to them and to regain the feeling of being part of a bigger company.

Source: Richard Nissen, The Virtual Office, 211 Piccadilly, London W1V 9DL Tel: 0171 917 2917.

Virtual teams

Virtual teamworking allows employees to collaborate from a variety of locations, using e-mail, groupware, the Intranet and video-conferencing These staff may be teleworkers, mobile workers or people working at opposite ends of the building or on different sites. There is no longer any need for members of a team to be physically located together, although the provision of office facilities described above under 'hot-desking' is important in allowing face-to-face meetings to take place.

This arrangement also permits employees to work with other employees in different organisations, allowing either agreements between organisations (see Thursday) or, at the least, networking on an informal basis. This may benefit the organisation in some circumstances, but it can also lead to worries about employee control and ownership of data (see Friday).

The computer-generated virtual office

An advanced application of the virtual office is being developed at British Telecom and the US National Institute of Standards and Technology. Their idea is to bring the look of a conventional office onto a PC screen so that you can create your own office space and needs whenever and wherever you wish. As well as allowing you to mimic your existing physical office, their technology permits you to 'walk' into adjoining offices to catch up with developments on various projects, and to 'visit' other buildings such as the bank or the library and carry out an appropriate task. This pushes the virtual organisation fully into the realms of virtual reality.

A further interesting concept being developed by the Mitsubishi Electronic Research Laboratory in Massachusetts is the *electronic meeting room* where matchstick figures sitting in a virtual meeting room depict the actions of the meeting's real participants. It is envisaged that the latter, seated in their various locations, will either wear jackets with sensors attached or have simple video cameras around them so that their body language can be transferred onto their corresponding matchstick figures on screen.

These developments may seem horrific to some, but the technologies are nonetheless being devised and tested as practical applications and viable alternatives to the way work has been done until now.

The benefits and problems associated with the virtual office

The benefits
- Work needing concentration can be done in isolation, and time at the office can be used for human interaction.
- There is an increase in productivity – typically quoted at between 30% and 50%.
- Workers save on commuting time and costs, with knock-on environmental benefits.
- Workers enjoy greater flexibility.
- Employers incur lower office costs, as savings of 25–30% can be made on office space.
- Teamworking is facilitated between people in different locations.
- Employees are able to spend more time with customers.
- People unable to take up normal office employment in standard office hours can be recruited.
- Labour markets in a wider geographic area can be tapped.

The problems
- Management may fear difficulties in controlling an 'invisible' workforce.
- Unless lines of communication are clear, there is a problem in ensuring that remote staff understand corporate goals and retain a sense of loyalty, and it is difficult to maintain a sense of cohesion.
- Managers may resent the loss of their own space with its accompanying status.
- Remote working can lead to a feeling of social isolation; many employees therefore prefer to work in a traditional office as it represents a social milieu as well as a workplace.
- There is a danger, particularly for young people entering work, that social skills will not be developed sufficiently.
- Employees may view homeworking as a solution to childcare problems.
- The virtual office cannot be implemented overnight because all concerned must have a familiarity with the enabling technologies, and therefore time must be put aside for familiarisation, practice and continuing training.

Summary

Today we have looked at changes in the way we work within an organisation. Tomorrow we shall consider how firms can further exploit technology and changing organisational concepts to create fluid, informal relationships with other companies to exploit market opportunities.

The emerging organisational model

Today, we shall see how organisations are looking outside their own four walls to form collaborative agreements, in the form of partnerships, strategic alliances and networks. Such agreements allow firms to take advantage of market opportunities, acquire new expertise and respond more quickly to the customer. They also constitute further examples of the virtual organisation.

We shall look at various aspects of the emerging virtual organisation in terms of:

- partnerships
- strategic alliances
- where alliances go wrong
- a network model
- the extreme form of virtual organisation

Partnerships

Growth
Numbers of both partnerships and inter-organisational alliances between large, medium and small companies have been steadily growing over the last 20 years both nationally and internationally. Behind this growth have been the continual search for competitive advantage and the need to win new customers under conditions of increasing market turbulence.

The traditional form of partnership took the shape of a joint venture between two organisations to form a new business that could be run separately by either party. Such a partnership would have resulted from development phases involving activities such as forming a negotiating team to hammer out new structures, control methods and financial arrangements; coming to an agreement on resource inputs and procedures; and establishing termination clauses.

Disadvantages of traditional partnerships
The process of forming a joint venture thus took time, imposing medium- to long-term planning on both parties. When the parties involved in such a venture numbered three, ten, twenty or more, the emerging consortium was all the more complex, requiring even more structures, procedures and control methods. Recently, it has been recognised that such a process may be too unwieldy and slow-moving to match the needs of fast-changing markets. More flexible forms of collaboration to emerge are those agreements to cooperate which, like partnerships, result from a recognition that both parties will enjoy better opportunities by working together rather than apart in the

marketplace, but which are more agile in that the partners can work on projects without the need to form a new enterprise. It is not so much a new business as a sharing of resources to adapt and improve old business.

Strategic alliances

Strategic alliances are networks of partners working remotely but united in purpose. Such a purpose may be short-term, for example, to improve market share for existing products. Here, the project will require partners with expertise in packaging, promotion and pricing in order to vary the product for those new markets to which one or some of the alliance partners will have access.

On the other hand, the unifying purpose may be longer-term, such as when markets have become increasingly segmented through a growth in customer preferences. This encourages the alliance to develop and pursue new strengths or core competencies in product innovation or regeneration, or greater production efficiency.

Forming alliances with other partners means acknowledging that the key to competitive advantage is not cast in stone but is changeable, and that linking together with outsiders will create more opportunities than will be created by working in isolation. It means recognising the need to:

- collaborate, because one organisation on its own, no matter how big, cannot contain all the resources and skills required to take on new market opportunities independently
- maintain the economies of scale needed by high-volume and low-cost production, not by increasing overheads but by sharing
- encourage a new form of control based on cooperation and trust
- add value by grouping together with others to form a new whole which is greater than the sum of its parts.

The organisations in an alliance are not physically relocated, nor do people spend the entirety of their time travelling the globe to meet. Alliances can be seen as a pattern of linkages, connections or interactions between participating organisations and individuals. Working from remote locations, people communicate by e-mail, voice-mail and video-conference as well as face-to-face. Teams come together composed of people who:

- have never met each other, and will probably meet only rarely
- communicate with each other in a variety of ways
- will be working on various projects at the same time

- carry out different functions and come from different levels, as well as from different organisations and different locations.

These alliances have been described as virtual organisations, and the key activity here is the free flow of information among the participating organisations in order to stimulate individual and organisational learning. The success of the alliance depends largely on *what* knowledge is acquired from the others, and new importance is also attached not only to how information is conveyed – its form of transfer, frequency, reliability and speed – but also to how information is received – ideally, with acceptance, trust, belief and an ability to respond.

Where alliances go wrong

Research by Booz-Allen & Hamilton has shown that although top firms in the USA draw a growing proportion of their revenue from alliances, many such collaborations fail. There are a number of reasons for this.

- *Implementation problems:* cultural incompatibility and leadership struggles tend to slow the development down. Interdependence can be harder for some to come to terms with than for others; former control methods can be difficult to shed, and decision-making can be hampered by the need to refer back to 'HQ'.
- *A lack of trust:* too often, sufficient understanding is not reached on who does what and who counts where, and this leads to aggression between the organisations.

- *Choice of partner:* a strong partnership cannot be made between two weak organisations, or where one partner is stronger than the others, or where inbred notions of competition may be difficult to set aside.

In the Harvard Business Review, Chesborough and Teece argue that the key question for the virtual organisation is how to organise for innovation. The answer depends on the type of information which the alliance needs in order to move forward. When information is publicly accessible and has become standardised in rules, regulations, patents and specifications, then it is more easily transferable and ready for commercial application. When, however, that information is relatively new, has not yet found expression in transferable codes and is itself innovative, then it will not necessarily be in the owners' best interests, or even capability, to pass it on. When a stronger network partner has invested more in its core competencies than others, control may be consciously or unconsciously exerted by withholding key elements of information. When the nature of cooperation requires such information-sharing across an entire network, this can cause imbalances.

A network model

Networks of organisations are still evolving, and there is as yet no ideal form or structure. Because of this continuing evolution, commentators have sought to define a *model* for such collaborations in the attempt to understand the best route for organisational developments.

Charles Handy sees the network as a federation whose component parts are naturally dispersed and whose interdependence lies in common, flexible rules of conduct. In a federation, it is recognised that people have not just one allegiance but several. Here, leadership depends on getting things right for all points in the network; authority has to be earned; people have to own their work, and what is good for the individual should be good for the whole. The virtual organisation as a federation:

- allows people to do things their own way provided it is in the common interest
- enables people to be well-informed in order to interpret and advance that common interest
- balances power among those at the centre and those at the edge
- obviates the need for people to share the same office or co-locate, because other ways of getting information to people at their workplace are more effective

- hinges on the concept of *subsidiarity* which involves not 'handing out' or delegating power but ruling and unifying only with the consent and agreement of equal partners
- is managed by common goals, and by consent on who does what and whose authority counts where
- allows organisations to appear big and yet be small at the same time: big for financing new research programmes and penetrating new markets; small for flexibility, innovation and quick response to change.

So how can a network benefit both from the agility of smaller organisations and the resources of larger ones? If many alliances break up after they have outlived their purpose, why not build the notion of transience into the nature of the relationship from the beginning? This leaves room for an even more flexible form of network organisation to come together at need and then disperse when that need has been achieved – the virtual organisation in its most extreme form.

The extreme form of virtual organisation

If change is continuous, then it is unlikely that networks with static, permanent features will succeed beyond a certain period of time. There will come, sooner or later, the search for different knowledge, different assets, capabilities and skills which will drive some partners in a current collaboration to look for *new* relationships. The network, set up to provide more flexibility over fixed organisational structures, will itself also have to keep evolving, forming new relationships and dissolving others. As information is spread to every part of the network, some partners will learn more, and faster, than others. This learning will push the network in various directions, closing off those which are no longer needed. If the capacity for replacing and renewing damaged, tired or obsolete parts of the network is not built in from the beginning, then it is not surprising that many alliances collapse.

The concept of the virtual organisation depends on 'real' organisations forming new organisational and individual relationships to meet a market opportunity. An organisation can be a partner in several virtual organisations at the same time.

Virtual partners
Membership of a virtual organisation does not focus on control structures and termination clauses but recognises the need for different strengths, and therefore different relationships, at different times. A virtual organisation can be open-ended, with partners joining and leaving as opportunities occur, disappear or are achieved. The success of the virtual organisation lies in the ability of its partner-members to trust each other to share methodologies for

tackling opportunities that no-one of them could take on on its own.

Case study: The Burton Morris Consultancy

The Burton Morris Consultancy (BMC) offers a writing service to organisations. This includes writing material into plain English and other copywriting. The company also produces material on management and organisations.

BMC is a virtual organisation in a number of key respects:

- It has a small number of core staff – three at BMC's office.
- It contracts teams of people to work on projects as and when they are needed: end of project means end of contract.
- These teams are spread around the UK and are made up of specialists appropriate to the demand.
- They are linked by telecommunications: everyone works on a Mac, has a modem, and stays in regular contact by phone.

To the client, the joins don't show. Although the client knows the team is dispersed and brought together only for the project, it feels cohesive, with each team member sharing the same set of values and commitment to doing things the BMC way. A virtual organisation must actually feel like a real organisation to the customer – a flesh-and-blood group of people pulling together, with a focal person who takes responsibility. This is how it works:

An organisation contracted BMC to redraft 150 customer letters into plain English. BMC put a team together to do the job: a specialist full-time plain-English writer, an editor, a proofreader, a legal specialist to check for legal accuracy and a project manager to liaise with the client and make sure that the project moved through on time. The project manager worked at BMC's office, while the rest worked from home. The director of BMC and the project manager met the client and agreed requirements. They then briefed other members of the team. The writer wrote the new letters and sent the text through to BMC by modem, the project manager read and suggested changes, the lawyer checked for legal issues, the writer made the changes, and the proofreader checked the results.

Three weeks later, the client received the 150 letters. At this stage, the writer and lawyer had finished their work. The client then sent through revisions, the project manager hired an inputter to input them into the text, the proofreader checked them and the director read them all through before they were sent off. One happy client, one trouble-free job for them. Goodbye team, hello new team for the next job.

Source: Steve Morris, The Burton Morris Consultancy, 8 Campbell Road, London W7 3EA. Tel: 0181 566 4874.

If virtual organisations have little or no structure, then the organisational core needs both a method of identifying pre-qualification assets which members can contribute, and to recognise the incentives and outcomes that members will require.

The success of a virtual organisation lies in the relationships between the partners, the degree of trust they have in each other, their mutual commitment to the form of collaboration and the flexibility of attitude they bring to the relationship. Some partner guidelines have already emerged:

- Each partner must contribute a clearly identifiable asset or strength to the organisation.
- Core skills or competencies must be complementary, not identical, and preferably not overlapping.

- Partners have to be adaptable and sensitive to the cultural and organisational differences between them.
- The will to cooperate must be at least as important as any contractual agreements because mistakes will happen and misunderstandings will occur.

A key challenge in the formation of a virtual relationship is to allow each partner access to the others' skills and knowledge. This does not mean giving up every piece of proprietary or confidential information, but it does mean coming to terms on what each partner can and should contribute, and working in an open and trusting manner. Research has shown that organisations which are less formal, more flexible, delayered, empowered and customer-focused, and which have identified their core competencies, are more likely to be successful in virtual networks than those which are rigid bureaucracies.

There may be a preference for small or medium-sized rather than large partners; early evidence thus shows that size may be important to the notion of real trust.

Case study: Reuters Holdings

When Greg Garrison of Reuters Holdings needed a constantly
evolving and changing team of experts to work on new user
interfaces for the financial information services provided by
Reuters, he created a virtual team by bringing in top talent from
12 companies around the world. The team shrinks and grows
and changes its skills composition according to the work needed.
Some of the members work on-site in the Reuters London office
and others participate remotely using e-mail, fax and telephone.
Along with the expertise they have, each member also brings
access to the skills pool of the companies to which they belong.

This collaborative agreement was facilitated by persuading the
firms involved to sign non-disclosure contracts not just with
Reuters but also with each other. It is expensive, with Reuters
paying between £300 and £500 a day per person. Savings on
recruitment costs, staff benefits and other overheads mean,
however, that Greg Garrison is paying a premium of only 8-15%
above the market rate and he can use high calibre staff as and
when he needs them.

Source: Adapted from the *Financial Times*, 16 November 1994, p.20.

Summary

With the formation and dissolution of virtual organisations,
the worker can work for the parent organisation and others
on many projects at the same time, from the office or home,
on a just-in-time basis. Electronic connectivity brings
people together *when* they need to work together. In this
sense the virtual organisation becomes both dynamic and
transient, real for the time but existing only temporarily to
meet a demand. Tomorrow we shall look at the human
implications of virtual working.

The human dimension

Virtuality has enormous implications for employees, organisations and society as a whole. Today we consider some of the human issues. These include:

- management control
- managing trust
- career management
- commitment and loyalty
- the impact on society

Management control

While the growth of internal and external computer networks has advantages for organisations, it also raises serious questions for management control. There are three particular areas of concern:

1 *The facilitation of personal networking.* The informal relationships which these networks foster can be pools of opportunity for the organisation but they can also lead to abuse: time-wasting, for example, or more seriously, the leaking of corporate secrets. How can it be ensured that users of networks are working towards the strategic aims of the organisation, or at least are not in conflict with them?

2 *The creation of an information democracy.* If more and more information is shared within and between organisations, it becomes increasingly possible for employees to make their own judgements and to challenge those of others. What form does authority now

take? How is it to be maintained? What kind of
leadership will be appropriate?

3 *The blurring of organisational boundaries.* Managers are
increasingly asked to control people who lie beyond their
team, department or even organisation. How, in Charles
Handy's words, do you manage people whom you do not
see at work?

The answers to these questions may be found in the
emerging theories stressing the need for greater trust
between employer and employee.

Managing trust

Commentators agree that, in order to exploit the full
capabilities of virtuality, the organisation needs to trust its
employees. One of the foremost writers in this area, whom
we have already mentioned, is Charles Handy. He suggests
several principles for managing trust, and the following
points are based on his work:

1 *Managers should have small spans of control.* It is difficult to trust those whom you do not know well, and it is hard to know over 50 people well. Larger spans of control, however, have often become the norm in flatter organisations and to overcome some of the problems this brings, organisations are turning to '360 degree' appraisal systems. Here, instead of being appraised solely by superiors, employees are appraised by their peers, and sometimes even by their subordinates and customers. The idea is that an all-round appraisal is given, by those who are closest.

2 *Freedom of action must be contained within boundaries.* While empowerment (see Monday) releases employee energy and responsibility and frees staff from rigid rules, guidelines for behaviour are still needed. Managers need to define the goals and limits of an activity, have confidence in the ability of the employee to do the job, and then let them get on with it.

3 *Trust must be tough.* Empowerment encompasses the need to allow employees the freedom to make mistakes. This must be balanced, however, by the ability to let go of people who do not live up to expectations or who can no longer be relied upon: the alternative would be to reintroduce checking and control procedures, and this would upset the system of trust that has been built up. In the virtual organisation, extra care over recruitment and promotion becomes ever more important.

4 *Commitment is vital.* A key building block of trust is to have confidence that employees are committed to the organisation's goals. Apart from redefining relationships with individual employees, the organisation must also attempt to bond the whole together. Ways of doing this include participation in the collective formulation of vision and mission statements, campaigns for quality and excellence, and senior managers leading by example.

5 *Personal contact must be maintained.* Everyone knows that it is much easier to deal with people at a distance when you have already met them face-to-face: the personal touch oils the wheels of business. This becomes even more important in the virtual organisation where more and more work is done remotely. Get-togethers become principally social occasions where people meet and get to know one another and where corporate goals and behaviour can be reinforced, while the real work is done virtually, at a distance.

6 *Leaders are still needed.* The virtual organisation will be dependent on the membership of different specialists, and the managers' skills will be of no less or more value than those of their professional colleagues in, for example, engineering, finance or medicine. Every member of the team will have to be a leader at those times when the others have to rely on that member's knowledge and experience. Everyone, however, will also have to be a follower at some point too.

Case study: the Institute of Management

The Institute of Management runs a variety of training courses for its members. The course presenters, in the main, are not Institute staff, and workshops are held in several locations. The Short Course Administration Department maintains contact and communication in a number of ways:

- A regular newsletter keeps presenters in touch with the centre and with each other.
- Delegate feedback forms are analysed, and the results are sent back to the presenters.
- There is regular contact between the centre and presenters by telephone, letter and fax.
- General guidelines for course leadership are provided which include advice on how to present the Institute. The presenters in turn feed back ideas on best practice based on their experiences from working with other organisations.

The Institute goes beyond staying in touch with distance-based associates by building relationships which foster mutual commitment and trust.

- It hosts a presenters' day in Corby which combines a social meeting with training.
- Institute staff attend various courses, including all new programmes.
- Presenters are given a free place on other courses of their choice for professional interest and development.
- Associates are encouraged to make use of the Institute's Management Information Centre as a development resource.

Source: Institute of Management. Tel: 01536 204222.

Career management

An increasingly important dilemma for organisations is the problem of how to develop and reward individuals when delayering, teamworking and empowerment have led to the removal of career structures. This has been a shock for the majority of today's workers who have been brought up to work for, and be rewarded by, advancement up the organisation, and it is a serious motivational issue for employers. Organisations are struggling to devise ways of developing employee careers within flatter structures and to replace traditional pay packages based on status with reward systems which reflect the new team-based environment and the skills and behaviours which are required today.

Various solutions have been attempted including secondment and job rotation, which offer opportunities for employees to expand their capability through widening their work experience beyond former boundaries, and dual career ladders where specialists such as salespeople, engineers and financial analysts can be rewarded and promoted in parallel with their managerial colleagues without becoming managers themselves. One vital role that organisations have, however, is to encourage employees to define their own career expectations, and to support them in developing the skills and attributes which will enhance their employability. Having said that, employees must take, and are taking, increasing responsibility for their own career development. The following recommendations for individuals were made in an Institute of Management/ Clerical Medical Investment survey report on the nature and structure of managerial work in the post-recession economy, entitled *Survival of the Fittest:*

- *Change:* individuals must be prepared for change and embrace it. Opportunities for personal development and career advancement should be actively sought.
- *Stress:* it is essential that stress levels be managed. Individuals must learn to measure their susceptibility to stress, acknowledge its presence and act to reduce it.
- *Self-employment:* moves towards flexible working and the increasing trend towards interim management and outsourcing open up opportunities for managers to take greater control over whom they work for and when and how they work.
- *Employability:* individuals should focus on a range of transferable skills. These include: computer literacy, interpersonal skills, communication techniques, languages, teamworking, negotiation, financial management and strategic analysis.
- *Training:* individuals must become more proactive in ensuring they are trained in the skills appropriate to future job markets. Traditional, organisation-based training may only reinforce a specific corporate practice and culture and will not be sufficient to ensure the continuing competitiveness of individuals in the market for jobs.
- *Time management:* managers must learn to prioritise their work. Effective time management enables individuals to improve their efficiency, thus maximising organisational benefits. It is equally important to reserve time for life outside work.
- *Continuing Professional Development:* CPD encourages managers to develop their own competencies, and provides planning for, and a structure to, their career development, which may involve some level of personal investment of time, energy and money. It should be embraced by all managers.

Personal development planning checklist

1 Find out where you are. Start with a self-assessment exercise in terms of skills, employment, qualifications, responsibilities and achievements. This will form your current skills and knowledge base against which you can move forward.

2 Identify your career goals. Ask where you want to be in the future, in both the short and longer term. Are you likely to remain in full-time managerial employment, or do you see yourself running your own business? Map out the steps that will allow you to reach your goal(s). Be realistic: development is usually incremental.

3 Map your current profile against these goals and take responsibility for identifying and assessing your development needs. These vary over time, and may arise from:

- a new or changed job role
- new technology or management techniques
- formal performance-appraisal systems
- self-assessment or periodic review.

List the skills or knowledge you will need to acquire, update or improve.

4 Convert development needs into learning objectives. For each of the gaps you have identified, set yourself development objectives. These need to be SMART: Specific, Measurable, Achievable, Realistic and Timely. There must be an element of challenge in them, but they must also be attainable within a realistic time-frame. You will need to consider:

- your learning style – mover, shaker or observer, or a preference for trial and error
- the resources available – organisational, community, personal

- the processes required – educational programmes, development activities, skills training.

Don't interpret 'development' too narrowly and restrict yourself to conventional training activities; don't be afraid of asking for help, and don't force yourself down a particular route because you think it is expected.

5 Monitor your progress. Record not only your planned intentions but also your development experiences and their outcomes, both positive and negative. Your personal evaluation and reflections on learning experiences are essential.

6 Revise and update the plan. Review your plan at least once a year. Reassess your goals honestly and ensure they are still valid. Revisit your learning objectives and update them to take account of organisational and technological changes.

Commitment and loyalty

As employees develop their skills and increase their knowledge, they become more and more valuable to the information-based organisation. They are therefore likely to

look for the highest bidder for their services and then join,
perhaps, a competitor firm. While organisations are looking
to see how they can retain their human assets, the picture is
complicated by two issues:

1 Loyalty was heavily damaged by the downsizings of the
  last decade. Having shed it unthinkingly, companies are
  starting to realise that it is valuable, but difficult to restore.
2 The people who worked for one company for 40 years
  have been replaced by individuals who value loyalty to
  their profession or team above that of the organisation,
  and who value outside interests as highly as their work.

A new psychological contract (an unwritten agreement on
what employees and organisations expect from each other)
is needed to replace the old one which worked on the
understanding that the employee would stay committed
and loyal in return for job security, a suitable job, annual
pay increases and promotion prospects. Most suggestions
for a renewed contract acknowledge the removal of job
security but emphasise the need for the organisation to
help its employees to develop skills and experience, to
involve them to some extent in the management of the
business, to offer interesting work and to give rewards that
reflect their contribution.

The impact on society

Virtuality will not only have an impact on individuals and
organisations, it will also contribute towards re-shaping
society. While virtuality embraces the growing number of
skilled, knowledge workers, there is a danger of bypassing
the unskilled and the long-term unemployed and excluding

them from the benefits that virtuality is bringing. These people must also be helped to acquire the skills which organisations will need in the future, and to play a full and active role in the social economy. Businesses have a social as well as an economic responsibility.

Where organisations have reduced their core workforce and turned to contract workers, they have contributed to the general feeling of insecurity which in turn affects the national economy. People who are made redundant, worried about losing their job, or wondering where their next contract is coming from are reluctant to spend money on goods and services. One of the greatest concerns about virtuality is that organisations will want to accelerate this trend towards less secure work patterns. If they do, they may come across resistance in their search for high-quality staff who are prepared to work on short-term contracts. Most people still want a long-term, secure job unless they have no choice, because other social, domestic and financial considerations, such as paying off a mortgage and raising a family, will not have changed. On the other hand, will the new work patterns continue to affect the home and the family with a longer-term and a deeper-rooted impact than before?

Summary

Today we have raised some of the issues associated with virtuality. There are currently many questions but few answers:

- How can organisations retain the commitment and loyalty of individuals when there are no longer jobs for life?
- How can managers control workers whom they do not often meet and whose activities are not always visible?
- How can personal contacts be maintained in an age of remote working?
- What will give people the confidence to become the flexible contract workers that organisations need?
- How can the majority – not just the minority – benefit from virtuality?

Tomorrow we look at the steps that organisations can take in preparing for an uncertain future.

Preparing for the future

Today we consider the implications of the virtual organisation, and assess what organisations need to do to prepare for the future. We shall look at various aspects of the virtual organisation, including:

- the different elements of virtuality
- when virtuality may not be the answer
- benefits of the virtual organisation
- checklist: preparing for the future

Different elements of virtuality

The concept of the virtual organisation is still evolving. For some it means being physically 'not there', but using communication technologies linked to computer databases, electronic diaries and workgroups, giving full service value as if someone were there all the time.

For others, virtuality means slimming down, reorganising around core competencies to network with and achieve interdependence with others for projects which do not require permanent new structures.

Whatever the concept of virtuality, it relies on two key factors:

1 New ways of managing people, with empowerment and trust driving organisational relationships.
2 The movement of electronic information across time and space, in cyberspace, to provide new functionality and new capability.

Not all organisations will want, or need, to become virtual organisations in the future. The virtual organisation will rely, for its existence, on the passage, manipulation and exploitation of electronic data in all its forms – text, voice, graphics, image, video – regardless of place or time. Although that information may represent, and even control, physical resources, in many cases it will not be able to replace them altogether. Electronic cash transfer may replace the physical movement of money but not money itself. Computer-aided design may provide the illusion of the real thing but not the thing itself.

When virtuality may not be the answer

There are organisational and market conditions when you may not want to take part in a virtual organisation, for example when:

• there is a lack of a strategic 'fit' with proposed partners, and incompatible management styles
• all the core competencies to take on a market project are

already in place
- trust and 'sharing' would be difficult to achieve
- there is a risk of sacrificing unique, hard-earned and high-value knowledge
- the project – and its outcome – has been ill-defined.

In short, there may be greater advantage to staying out of a relationship and waiting and seeing, rather than taking part. If there are well-defined reasons for opting out of the virtual organisation, what are the benefits of opting in?

Benefits of the virtual organisation

If the organisation has its own unique strengths which it is prepared to contribute, and if it is prepared to take risks, the virtual organisation can:

- benefit from expertise in different countries, operating across time zones
- lead to an opportunity for organisations to reconfigure themselves without having to restructure or shed jobs
- enable a small business to retain its agility but harness the resources for development, economies of scale and the market penetration of much larger organisations
- reduce the burden of capital resourcing by sharing
- reduce time to market and increase the pace of growth in ways that an individual business could not do on its own
- take advantage of complementary partner skills to focus on customer opportunities
- lead to excellence as each organisation concentrates on what it is best at.

On the one hand, virtuality has yet to demonstrate proven benefits over time. On the other hand, it is arguable that organisations cannot afford not to look at new ways of reorganising work, because:

- investing in people development has been proven to contribute to profitability for the organisation and the individual alike
- collaboration can reduce costs and increase market potential
- communication technologies can reduce costs and increase effectiveness.

Earlier in the week, we proposed that the strands of change affecting markets and technologies were impacting on the workplace. As the future of business and work is uncertain, it is important that organisations reconsider their position to see if aspects of virtuality are suitable, and to see how far they need to adapt to different ways of reshaping the organisation.

We shall conclude with the steps involved in this exercise.

Checklist: preparing for the future

1 *Take account of the changing market place.* Take a good look at your organisation in relation to its industry sector and market position. Analyse where you are now and how you got there. Look at what others are doing to compete on value, service, innovation and design. How will you afford to access new markets, with controlled costs, and deliver higher quality, faster, to the customer?
2 *Determine where you want to be in the future.* It will be difficult not to remain locked into the thinking of the past if you do not have a clear vision of the future, and

planning how to get there may well mean rethinking the business you are in or adjusting the orthodoxies that have dominated before. Consider getting to grips with risk and uncertainty by questioning the way you manage, and by focusing resources on your strengths.

3 *Look at your organisation's processes.* Consider who are the key stakeholders, and look carefully at:

- your programmes for continuing improvement and development
- how information is generated, manipulated and used
- the way work is done in terms of cost-efficiencies, cost-effectiveness, adaptability and capability for rapid response
- whether authority is released to encourage initiative

4 *Identify core competencies.* Looking back to Monday, identify those key processes at which you are, or need to be, best, and therefore at those skills which you need to develop and improve. Remember that core competencies are not something to be adopted at will: they are the result of years of effort, and they need organising to get the best value from them.

5 *Beware of continual downsizing.* Try to work out where downsizing is taking you: slimmer may not mean fitter, and the key to the new ways of working is not resolved merely by reducing numbers. Downsizing should be the result of rethinking the organisation so as to tackle a new direction or achieve greater efficiencies. Beware also of fixed structures which are difficult to galvanise in fast-changing times. Think instead of more flexible structures which will allow you to pull resources together from inside and outside the organisation according to need.

6 *Consider new ways of working.* On Wednesday we looked at ways in which costs can be reduced and efficiencies improved. New ways of working will include minimising energy consumption as a matter of routine and reducing potential damage to the environment. They will also mean casting off old assumptions such as:

- bringing the worker to the office
- the belief that employees who are not seen are not to be trusted
- distance being a barrier to communication
- IT being a cost instead of an alternative.

7 *Take advantage of new communications technology.* The convergence of computing and telecommunications lies at the heart of the virtual organisation through the dimension of cyberspace. Organisations can benefit in incremental steps by using:

- laptop computers for mobility, and the portable office
- groupware or Intranet technology for information-sharing
- telecommunications as an alternative to travel.

Cyberspace may sound like a term from science fiction, but it is here and it increasingly enables what happens in the real world to be mirrored effectively. The key to moving forward is to learn from the mistakes, hype and promise of the past.

8 *Look for the right collaborators.* Look for partners where resources, skills and attitudes are complementary and gains are mutual. On Thursday, we looked at the concepts of federalism and subsidiarity – how what is right for the organisation should be right for the

individual, and vice versa. On the one hand, look for shared values; on the other, think why a proposed partner may be difficult to work with and trust.

9 *Manage people.* Yesterday, we looked at the implications of virtuality for the individual. Managing people is not merely step 9 but all of steps 1–10. It means taking action to ensure support, training and retraining, especially when the workforce is not located in one area and the risks of isolation are a real threat. As the workplace becomes dispersed, do not ignore the importance of human contact.

10 *Manage the paradoxes.* Finally, recognise that there will be just as many contradictions and paradoxes to manage in the future as in the past:

- Information is for sharing with others *and* it is key to the organisation's own development. Despite all the information resources available, managers will need greater capability than before for decision-making under uncertainty.
- Managing uncertainty means motivating in a risk environment *and* encouraging the individual to take initiatives – and control of their own development – at a time when traditional protections from insecurity are disappearing.
- Attaching importance to experience needs to be balanced with attaching importance to adapting and learning.
- Learning means recognising both that there are increasing amounts and types of information to absorb *and* that no-one can know it all. Fear of confessing ignorance will need replacing with continuing inquisitiveness.

- Managers will need to know when – *and* which kind of – electronic communications *are* to be used, and when they are not appropriate: *cybermania* is as dangerous as *cyberphobia.*

Technology and innovative management are providing more and more flexible answers – it is now important for organisations to get the questions right.

References and further reading

Barnatt, Christopher, (1995) 'Office space, cyberspace and virtual organization', *Journal of General Management*, vol. 30, no. 4 pp. 78–91

Byrne, John A., Brandt, Richard and Port, Otis, (1993) 'The virtual corporation: the company of the future will be the ultimate in adaptability', *International Business Week*, 8 February, no. 3292, pp. 36–41

Chesbrough, Henry W., and Teece, David J., (1996) 'When is virtual virtuous? Organizing for innovation', *Harvard Business Review*, vol. 74, no. 1, pp. 65–73

Davidow, William H., and Malone, Michael S, (1992) *'The virtual corporation'*, New York: HarperCollins

Handy, Charles, (1995) *Beyond Certainty: the Changing Worlds of Organisations*, London: Hutchinson

Society of Management Accountants of Canada, (1993) *Virtual Corporations: How Real?* Hamilton, Ontario: Society of Management Accountants of Canada